my *Book* Grade 1

Modules 9-10

Authors and Advisors

Alma Flor Ada • Kylene Beers • F. Isabel Campoy
Joyce Armstrong Carroll • Nathan Clemens
Anne Cunningham • Martha C. Hougen • Tyrone C. Howard
Elena Izquierdo • Carol Jago • Erik Palmer
Robert E. Probst • Shane Templeton • Julie Washington

Contributing Consultants

David Dockterman • Jill Eggleton

Printed in the U.S.A.

ISBN   978-0-358-46148-7

9 10   0607   29 28 27 26 25 24 23 22

4500859388

r1.21

MODULE 9

Grow, Plants, Grow!

🌱 **SCIENCE CONNECTION:** Plants and Gardens

Plant Pairs

POETRY

So You Want to Grow a Taco?

by Bridget Heos • illustrated by Daniele Fabbri

PROCEDURAL TEXT

Which Part Do We Eat?

by Katherine Ayres • illustrated by Hazel Quintanilla

POETRY

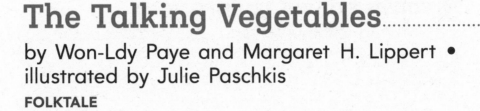

MODULE 10

Dare to Dream

Grow, Plants, Grow!

"The creation of a thousand forests is in one acorn."

—Ralph Waldo Emerson

? Essential Question

What do plants need to live and grow?

Get Curious
Video

Words About Plants and Gardens

Complete the Vocabulary Network to show what you
know about the words.

vegetation

Meaning: Plants, trees, and flowers are all kinds
of **vegetation**.

Synonyms and Antonyms	Drawing

absorb

Meaning: When things **absorb**, they soak something up or take it in.

Synonyms and Antonyms	Drawing

emerge

Meaning: When things **emerge**, they slowly come out where we can see them.

Synonyms and Antonyms	Drawing

READ Together

Plant Pairs

We see all kinds of plants around us. Find out **cool facts** and read **fun rhymes** about them!

Gardens are places where people grow plants, like vegetables and flowers.

Peter Piper

Peter Piper picked a peck of pickled peppers.
A peck of pickled peppers Peter Piper picked.
If Peter Piper picked a peck of pickled peppers,
Where's the peck of pickled peppers
Peter Piper picked?

Nursery Rhyme

April Showers

March winds
And April showers
Bring forth
May flowers.

Nursery Rhyme

Flowers need sunlight, soil, and water to grow. These flowers get water from rain.

I Had a Little Nut Tree

I had a little nut tree,
Nothing would it bear,
But a silver nutmeg
And a golden pear;
The king of Spain's daughter
Came to visit me,
And all for the sake
Of my little nut tree.

Nursery Rhyme

Trees give shade and food. This tree gives us great tasting walnuts to eat!

Prepare to Read

GENRE STUDY **Procedural texts** tell how to do or make something. Look for:

- directions to follow
- steps that show order
- ways pictures and words help you understand the text

SET A PURPOSE Think about the author's words as you read. Then decide, or **evaluate**, which details are the most important to help you understand the text.

POWER WORDS
terrific
ingredients
nutrients
soil
sow
harvest

Meet Bridget Heos.

SO YOU WANT TO GROW A TACO?

by Bridget Heos   illustrated by Daniele Fabbri

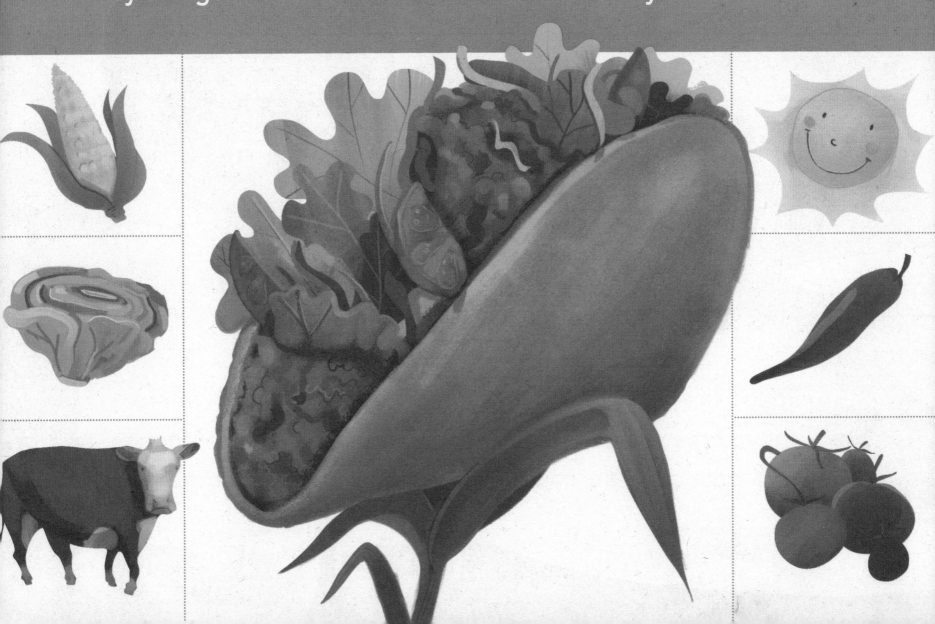

Tacos are terrific. But have you ever wondered where they come from? Like all food, they come from plants and animals. You could even grow a taco at home.

There's no such thing as a taco plant, of course.

But you can grow the ingredients.

For the tortillas, you'll need corn. For the meat, you'll need beef cows. The cheese will come from dairy cows.

You can grow the lettuce and tomatoes in your garden. Uh-oh. Maybe you should start small.

13

Let's say you want to make the corn tortillas. First you have to plant the corn. Did you know that the kernels that you eat are also the seeds planted to grow corn?

And you'll need to take care of the seeds. Think of it this way: We eat corn, but corn needs to eat, too! Corn food is sunlight, water, and the nutrients found in soil.

Find a sunny spot in your yard.

Line your garden with stones or a wooden frame. Then add soil.

Corn likes the soil to be really warm. Different parts of the country get warm at different times. Check the seed packet for the best time to plant where you live.

When you plant, remember that corn grows big and tall. And it doesn't like being crowded.

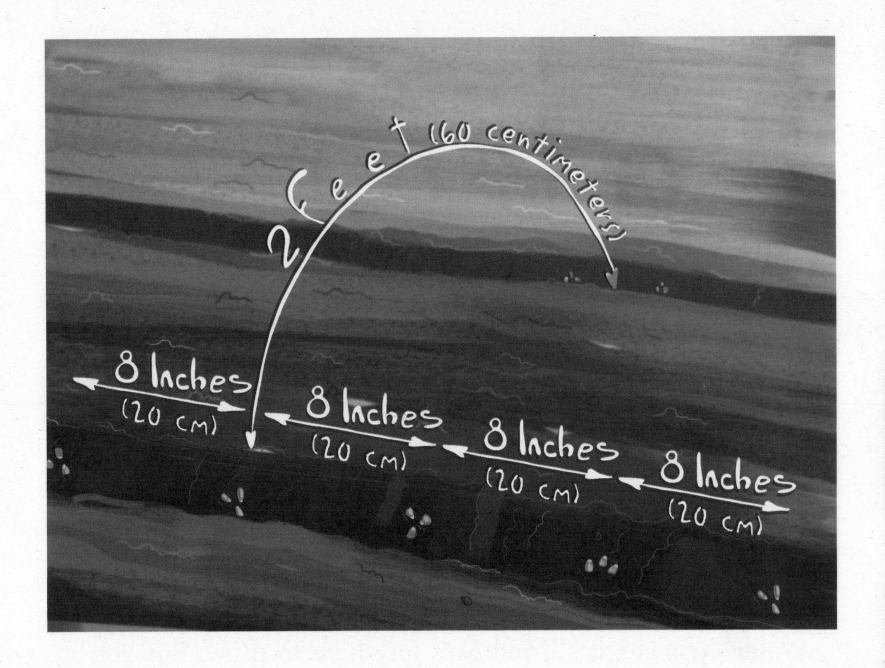

So leave plenty of space between rows. In each row, sow a few seeds into a small hole. Leave some space, and then plant a few more. Keep going along the row.

Water your seeds . . . and wait for them to grow. But you won't have to wait that long! Corn grows fast! Some people say that corn grows so fast that you can almost hear it grow.

To make tortillas, you need to let the ears dry on the stalk. Then harvest the corn, and hang it up to dry some more. Twist the dry corn so that it falls off the cob.

21

Then have a grown-up help you make the tortillas. There are a lot of steps!

Step 1: Boil the corn.

Step 2: Soak the corn.

Step 3: Grind the corn.

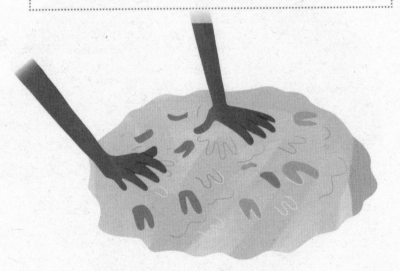

Step 4: Press the corn mush into a flat tortilla.

Step 5: Cook the tortilla.

Now it's taco time! Uh-oh! The tortillas are empty. What are you going to put in your tacos?

Don't worry. You can buy the meat, cheese, and salsa at the grocery store or a farmer's market.

And next year, you can add some of the taco toppings to your garden!

SO YOU WANT TO GROW A TACO?
by Bridget Heos   Illustrated by Daniele Fabbri

Turn and Talk

Use details from **So You Want to Grow a Taco?** to answer these questions with a partner.

1. **Evaluate** You read steps for making tortillas. Do they help you understand how to make tacos? Tell why or why not.

2. What important things does the boy learn about making tacos?

Talking Tip

Your ideas are important! Speak loudly and clearly as you share them.

I think that _____.

Write Directions

PROMPT How do you grow corn? Tell the steps.
Use the words, pictures, and diagrams in **So You
Want to Grow a Taco?** to get information.

PLAN First, write how to get the garden ready.
Then write notes about the rest of the steps.
Number the steps.

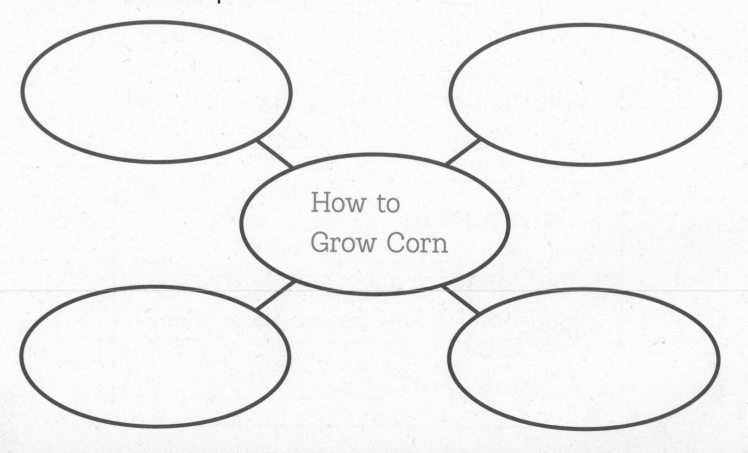

How to
Grow Corn

Turn and Talk

SO YOU WANT TO GROW A TACO?
by Bridget Heos   Illustrated by Daniele Fabbri

Use details from **So You Want to Grow a Taco?** to answer these questions with a partner.

1. **Evaluate** You read steps for making tortillas. Do they help you understand how to make tacos? Tell why or why not.

2. What important things does the boy learn about making tacos?

Talking Tip

Your ideas are important! Speak loudly and clearly as you share them.

I think that _____.

Write Directions

PROMPT How do you grow corn? Tell the steps. Use the words, pictures, and diagrams in **So You Want to Grow a Taco?** to get information.

PLAN First, write how to get the garden ready. Then write notes about the rest of the steps. Number the steps.

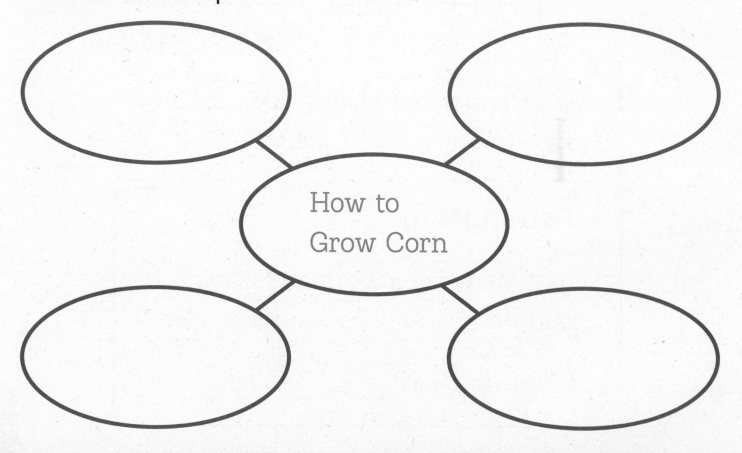

How to Grow Corn

WRITE Now write the steps for how to grow corn. Use your own words. Remember to:

- Tell how to get the garden ready as your first step.

- Use words like **first**, **next**, **then**, and **last** to help you explain the steps in order.

SO YOU WANT TO GROW A TACO?

_____

- -

_____

- -

_____

- -

_____

- -

_____

- -

_____

Prepare to Read

GENRE STUDY **Poetry** uses images, sounds, and rhythm to express ideas and feelings. Look for:

- rhyming words, repeated words
- a rhythm, or pattern of beats
- words that are fun to say

POWER WORDS

sturdy

cook

SET A PURPOSE As you read, stop and think if you don't understand something. Reread, look at the pictures, use what you already know, or ask yourself questions.

Meet Katherine Ayres.

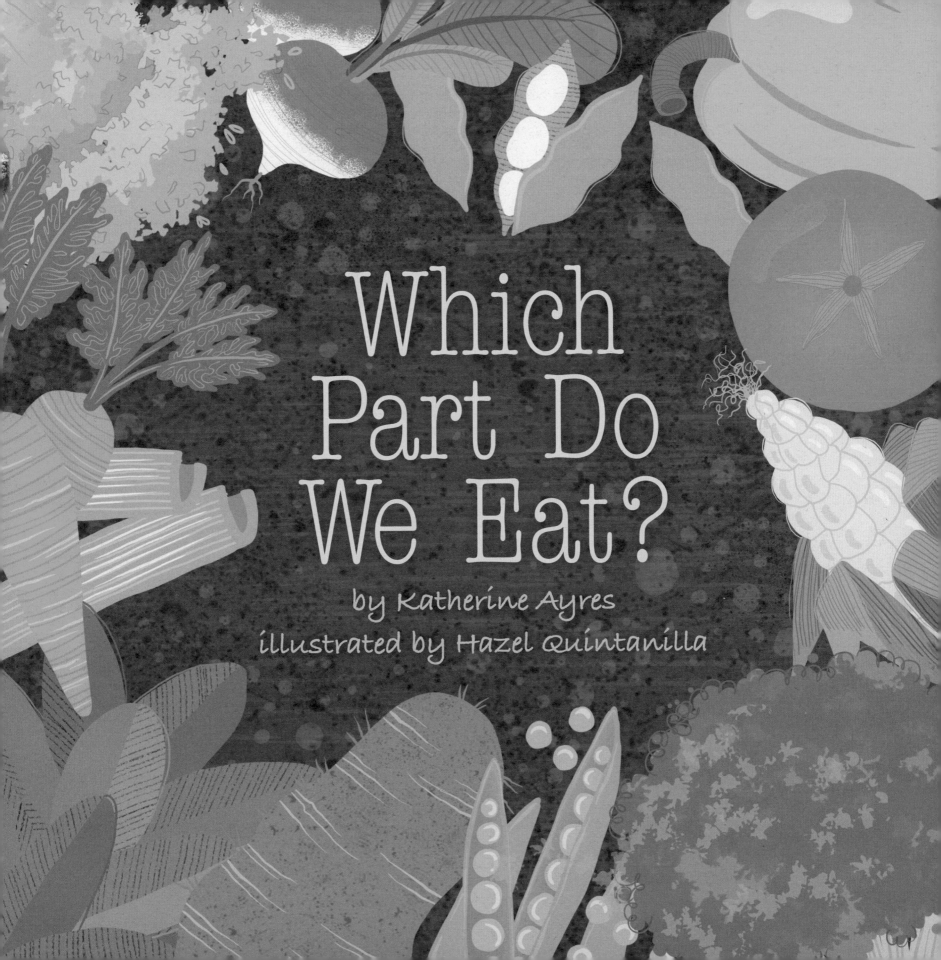

Which Part Do We Eat?

by Katherine Ayres

illustrated by Hazel Quintanilla

Let's run to the garden and pick us a treat!
But . . . which part do we eat?

Green beans, okras,
and peppers are odd . . .
We eat the pod.

Tomatoes and baby
zucchini are cute . . .
We eat the fruit.

Asparagus, celery?
What about them?
We eat the stem.

33

Lettuce, spinach, and chard?
I believe . . .
We eat the leaves.

Carrots and turnips
and yams aren't fruit . . .
We eat the root.

34

Tomatoes and baby
zucchini are cute . . .
We eat the fruit.

Asparagus, celery?
What about them?
We eat the stem.

33

Lettuce, spinach, and chard?
I believe . . .
We eat the leaves.

Carrots and turnips
and yams aren't fruit . . .
We eat the root.

34

Peas, corn, and lima beans
aren't weeds . . .
We eat the seeds.

Broccoli's filled
with vitamin power . . .
We eat the flower.

Stem, leaf, pod, fruit,
Flower, seed, or sturdy root—

Chop them and cook them and serve them on dishes.
Fresh crispy veggies are mighty delicious!

Use details from **Which Part Do We Eat?** to answer these questions with a partner.

1. **Monitor and Clarify** When you came to a part you did not understand, what did you do to figure it out?

2. Do you eat the same part of all vegetables, such as the stem? Explain.

Listening Tip

Listen carefully. Think about what your partner says about the topic.

Write a Description

PROMPT Choose two vegetables from **Which Part Do We Eat?** How are the vegetables alike? How are they different? Use information from the words and pictures.

PLAN First, write and draw how the two vegetables are alike and different.

Alike	Different

WRITE Now write sentences to compare the two vegetables. Describe how they are alike and how they are different. Remember to:

- Use words to describe color, size, shape, and other important details.

- Use complete sentences that begin with a capital letter and end with an end mark.

Prepare to Read

GENRE STUDY **Folktales** are stories from long ago that have been told over and over. Look for:

• animals that act and talk like people

• problems and resolutions

• a lesson that a character learns

POWER WORDS

pounding

smooth

delicious

stretched

SET A PURPOSE Read to understand events in the beginning, middle, and end. Use details in the words and pictures to help you. **Retell** the events in your own words.

Meet Won-Ldy Paye and Margaret H. Lippert.

The Talking Vegetables

retold by **Won-Ldy Paye** & **Margaret H. Lippert**

◙ illustrated by **Julie Paschkis** ◙

BAM! BAM! BAM!

"Who's pounding on my door so early in the morning?" Spider shouted.

"Your neighbors. It's time to clear the land for our village farm."

"Go away," said Spider. "I'm tired."

"But we need you," they said. "If everyone helps, there will be plenty of vegetables for all of us."

Spider yawned. "I don't need your vegetables. I have plenty of rice."

Everyone in the village walked down the road to a clearing in the forest.

Everyone except Spider.

They worked all day cutting down bushes, tearing out vines, and digging up roots. They raked smooth beds and built a waterway.

The next morning, the villagers came again to Spider's door.

BAM! BAM! BAM!

"Who's there?" Spider called.

"Your neighbors. Come help us plant the seeds."

"I said no, and I meant no!" shouted Spider. "Now go away!"

46

The villagers carried seeds to the farm and planted them in straight rows. They planted cassava, tomato, squash, pumpkin, cabbage, cucumber, pepper, and many different kinds of beans and greens.

A month later, the villagers knocked on Spider's door again.

BAM! BAM! BAM!

Spider opened his door and yelled, "What do you want now?"

"It's time to weed the farm," they answered.

"I didn't help before, and I'm **not** helping **now!**" Spider screamed. He slammed the door and went back to bed.

All day the villagers pulled weeds. Their knees hurt, their backs ached, and their arms were sore.

50

In time, the vegetables began
to ripen. The villagers picked what
they wanted.

51

One day Spider said to himself, "I'm getting tired of rice. Plain rice, day after day after day. I live here. I'm part of this village too. I'm going to pick myself some vegetables to go with my rice."

When Spider got to the farm he couldn't believe his eyes. Huge cucumbers lay on the ground. Giant pumpkins rested under green leaves. Juicy tomatoes hung from vines.

"Wow!" said Spider. "Those tomatoes look delicious. I'll just take one, or maybe two."

Spider reached out to pick a tomato from the nearest plant. The tomato shook itself and said, "What are you doing?"

Spider said, "Wha . . . ? A talking tomato?"

54

The tomato said, "Why do you think you can pick me when you didn't come to clear the land or plant my seeds or pull the weeds? Get out of here!"

Spider backed away. He looked around and said, "There are so many fat cucumbers on that vine. I'll just take one, or maybe two."

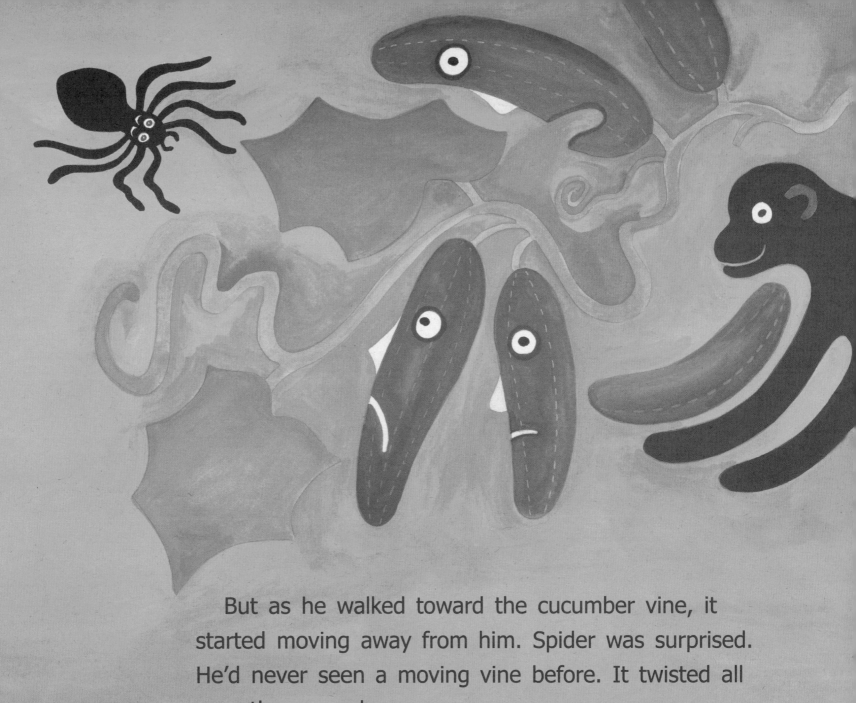

But as he walked toward the cucumber vine, it started moving away from him. Spider was surprised. He'd never seen a moving vine before. It twisted all over the ground.

"YOU can't pick us," said a cucumber. "You didn't clear the land. You didn't plant our seeds. You didn't pull the weeds."

Spider ran to the other side of the farm. Ahead he saw a perfect pumpkin—big enough, but not too big. "I'll just grab that pumpkin on my way out," he said. But he couldn't lift it. The pumpkin stuck to the ground.

He tugged and pulled, but the pumpkin wouldn't move. "You can't take me," the pumpkin said. "You didn't help make the farm. Go away!"

Spider tried to find his way out of the farm, but the vegetables reached up to grab him. Leaves covered his eyes. Stems stretched out to trip him.

60

Spider finally got free. He ran
all the way back to the village.

When he got home he was tired
and hungry. He put a pot of water
over the fire and boiled some rice.

That night he ate rice for dinner.

Plain rice!

Turn and Talk

Use details from **The Talking Vegetables** to answer these questions with a partner.

1. Retell Tell the story in your own words. Tell about the main events from the beginning, middle, and end.

2. What will Spider do the next time his neighbors ask for help? Tell why.

Talking Tip

Add your own idea to what your partner says. Be polite.

I like your idea.
My idea is _____.

Write a Dialogue

PROMPT Imagine that Spider tells his neighbors about the lesson he learns. What will he say? What will the neighbors say? Write a dialogue to add to **The Talking Vegetables**.

PLAN Write what lesson Spider learns. Tell why. Write what the characters say to each other.

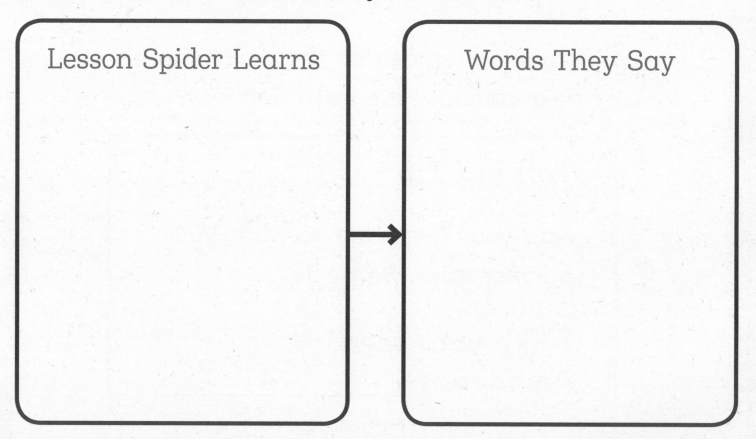

Lesson Spider Learns

Words They Say

WRITE Now write your dialogue between Spider and his neighbors! Then read your dialogue with a partner. Remember to:

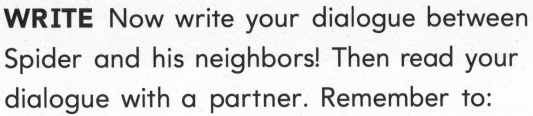

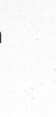

• Give reasons why Spider learns his lesson.

• Use quotation marks (" ") around the words the characters say.

Prepare to Read

GENRE STUDY ▶ **Poetry** uses images, sounds, and rhythm to express ideas and feelings. Look for:

- describing words
- alliteration, or a pattern of words with the same first sound
- the rhythm created by three lines with 5, 7, 5 syllables

SET A PURPOSE ▶ **Ask questions** before, during, and after you read to help you understand the text. Find evidence in the text and pictures to **answer** your questions.

POWER WORDS

indigo

wonder

syrup

juicy

ripe

Meet Pat Mora.

Yum!
¡MmMm!
¡Qué rico!

Americas' Sproutings

haiku by Pat Mora

illustrated by

Rafael López

BLUEBERRY

Fill your mouth with blue.
Share a bowl heaped with summer.
Chew indigo O.

CORN

Leaves sprout silk-snug house.
Smell grits, tortillas, corn bread.
Pass the butter, please.

PECAN

We crack hard, brown shells,
family munching, story time,
crunchy taste of fall.

PRICKLY PEAR

Red desert wonder.
Cactus fruit becomes syrup
and *dulces*. Surprise!

TOMATO

Round roly-poly
squirts seedy, juicy splatter.
Red bursts in your mouth.

Turn and Talk

Use details from **Yum! ¡MmMm! ¡Qué rico!** to answer these questions with a partner.

1. **Ask and Answer Questions** What questions did you ask yourself about the different foods before, during, and after reading? How did the questions help you understand the poems?

2. Which words help you imagine what the foods are like? Describe the foods.

Listening Tip

Look at your partner and listen politely. Think about what your partner is saying.

Write a Haiku

PROMPT Choose a food from **Yum! ¡MmMm!**
¡Qué rico! Write your own haiku about it!

PLAN First, draw and color a picture of the
food. Add details.

WRITE Now write a haiku about the food. Then show your picture and recite it for your classmates. Remember to:

- Use words to describe the food.

- Be sure your haiku has this pattern and rhythm: three lines with 5, 7, 5 syllables.

Prepare to View

GENRE STUDY **Videos** are short movies. Some videos give information. Others are for you to watch for enjoyment. Watch and listen for:

• the purpose of the video

• information about the topic

• the tone or mood of the video

SET A PURPOSE Find clues that the information is in **chronological order**, or in the order in which events happen. Think about how this helps you understand the information.

Build Background: Community Gardens

A Year
in the
Garden
by Brad Hiebert

As You View Notice how the video shows what happens first, next, and last to plants— really fast! Look for clues that the events are in order. Find out the steps a family follows to grow plants. How does having information in time order help you understand the video?

Turn and Talk

Use details from **A Year in the Garden** to answer these questions with a partner.

1. **Chronological Order** Tell the steps for planting a garden. Use the words **first**, **next**, and **last**.

2. How does the family feel about having a garden? Tell how you know.

Talking Tip

Wait for your turn to talk. Explain your ideas and feelings clearly.

I think that _____.

Let's Wrap Up!

Essential Question

What do plants need to live and grow?

....

Pick one of these activities to show what
you have learned about the topic.

1. Plan Your Garden

What would you grow in a
garden? Draw your garden
with all the different
kinds of plants. Then
explain to a partner
how you would take
care of your garden.

flower

tomato

leaves

stem

roots

2. Our Plant Book

Choose an interesting plant you have learned about. Draw it and label its parts. Write facts about it. Then put your page into a class book.

Word Challenge

Can you use the word absorb to tell about your plant?

My Notes

Dare to Dream

"I knew that whatever I set
my mind to do, I could do."

—Wilma Rudolph

? Essential Question

How can thinking in new ways help solve problems?

Get Curious
Video

Words About Thinking in New Ways

Complete the Vocabulary Network to show what you know about the words.

future
Meaning: The **future** is the time that has not happened yet.

Synonyms and Antonyms	Drawing

applaud

Meaning: When you **applaud** something, you clap or show that you like it in some other way.

Synonyms and Antonyms	Drawing

genius

Meaning: A **genius** is a very smart person.

Synonyms and Antonyms	Drawing

KIDS ARE INVENTORS, TOO!

Long ago, a boy named Chester had a problem. His ears were cold! Find out what he invented.

Chester Greenwood

Chester Greenwood invented a new kind of earmuffs when he was just a boy. It all started long ago, in 1873. Chester liked to ice-skate. There was just one problem. His ears got too cold!

He tried wrapping a scarf around his head. It was too itchy. That's when he got a great idea!

Ronald Greenwood wears old earmuffs invented by his great-grandfather.

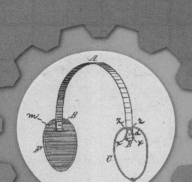

Next, he asked his grandmother to sew soft fur onto each loop.

Then Chester put his new invention on his head. His ears stayed warm. Chester's earmuffs worked!

Chester bent some metal wire to make a headband with two loops.

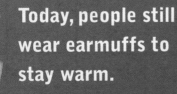

Today, people still wear earmuffs to stay warm.

Prepare to Read

GENRE STUDY **Realistic fiction** stories are made up but could happen in real life. Look for:

- characters who act and talk like real people
- settings that are real places
- events that could really happen

SET A PURPOSE Read to understand events in the beginning, middle, and end. Look for details in the words and pictures to help you. **Retell** the events in your own words.

POWER WORDS

floor

straight

designed

whole

real

model

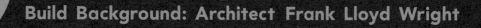

Build Background: Architect Frank Lloyd Wright

YOUNG FRANK
ARCHITECT

by Frank Viva

Young Frank's apartment is on the top floor of this tall building.

He is an architect.

He lives with his spotted dog, Eddie, and his grandpa, Old Frank, who is also an architect.

Young Frank makes things.

He uses anything he can get his hands on: macaroni, books, dishes, spoons, dogs . . . Dogs? Not Eddie! Yes, even Eddie. But only sometimes.

One morning, Young Frank made
a chair using toilet paper rolls.

"Hmm," said Old Frank,
"I don't think architects
make chairs. And you
can't really sit in this
one, can you?"

"I guess not," said
Young Frank.

He also made a skyscraper out of books.

"Hmm, buildings should be straight," said Old Frank, "not twisted and wiggly. Hey, are those MY books?"

Just before lunch, Young Frank designed a whole city.

"Hmm," said Old Frank, "cities are made one
building at a time and take hundreds of years."

At lunch, Young Frank said, "Grandpa, I'm not sure I want to be an architect anymore."

"Hmm," said Old Frank. "I know, let's go to the museum. I think it will be very good for you to see the work of some REAL architects. Don't you? Hmm?"

"I haven't been to the museum in years and years," said Old Frank.

"Me neither," said Young Frank.

99

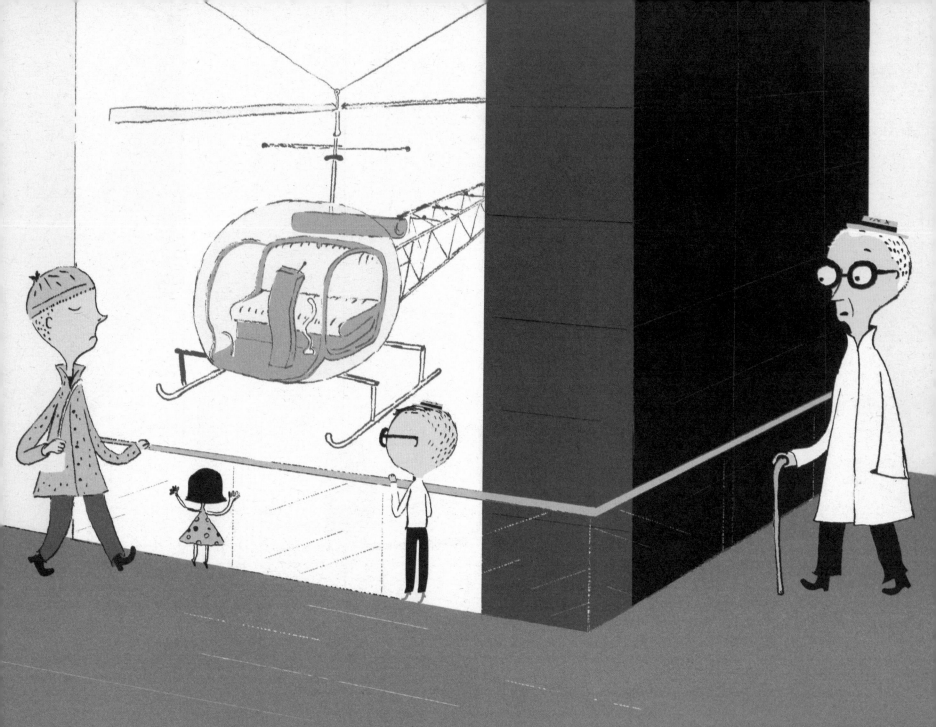

They saw lots of things, including . . .

A wiggly chair designed by an architect named Frank.

Old Frank looked at it sideways.

A twisted tower by an architect named Frank.

Old Frank cleaned his glasses.

They also saw a giant model of a whole city designed by another architect named Frank.

"Are all architects named Frank?" asked Young Frank.

"I don't think so," said Old Frank.

When they got home, Old Frank said, "Hmm, architects really do make chairs and twisted towers and cities, too. I guess I was wrong."

"That's okay, Grandpa," said Young Frank. "Even I don't know SOME things."

That evening, Young Frank and Old Frank made chairs.
Chairs with zigzags. Chairs with crazy legs.

And a little chair that was perfect for Eddie.

They made buildings of every shape and size.
Tall ones, fat ones, round ones, and one
made from chocolate chip cookies.

"Eddie! Don't eat the library," said Young Frank. "And please get back on your chair."

105

When they were done,
they had a whole city.

"Woof,"
 said Eddie.

"Shh, Eddie," said Young Frank.
"Stay until I tell you. Good boy!"

Later that night, when Young Frank was tucked in his bed, he felt a bit older—like a REAL architect.

For his part, Old Frank felt younger—and a little wiser.

"Woof,"
said Eddie.

108

 Turn and Talk

 YOUNG FRANK ARCHITECT
by Frank Viva

Use details from **Young Frank Architect** to answer these questions with a partner.

1. **Retell** Tell the story in your own words. Tell about the main events from the beginning, middle, and end.

2. Describe the different kinds of things architects do.

Talking Tip

Say your ideas. Speak clearly and not too fast or too slow.

I think that _____.

Write an Explanation

PROMPT Pick one of the things Young Frank makes in the story. How do you think he makes it? Explain the steps.

PLAN First, write or draw the materials Young Frank uses and what he makes. Use details from **Young Frank Architect**.

Materials He Uses

He uses tolet paper rolls and Krbored.

What He Makes

Frank makes a city.

WRITE Now write the steps Young Frank follows to make the thing. Remember to:

- Write the steps in order.

- Use action verbs and words that describe details, like sizes, shapes, and colors.

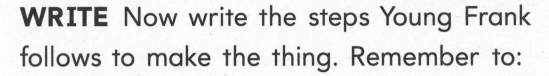

First he made a chia
with tolet paper. Then
he derw a city.

Prepare to Read

GENRE STUDY ▸ **Realistic fiction** stories are made up but could happen in real life. Look for:

- characters who act and talk like real people
- events that could really happen
- ways pictures and words help you understand the story

SET A PURPOSE ▸ Read to make smart guesses, or **inferences**, about things the author does not say. Use what you know and clues in the text and pictures.

POWER WORDS

artist
gallery
mural
rummaged

Meet Peter H. Reynolds.

Sky Color

by Peter H. Reynolds

Marisol was an artist.
She loved to draw and paint,
and she even had her very
own art gallery.

Not all her art hung in a gallery.
Much of it she shared
with the world.

She painted posters
to share ideas she
believed in.

At school, Marisol was famous for
her creative clothes, her box of art supplies,
and her belief that everybody was an artist.

Yes, Marisol was an artist through and through. So, when her teacher told the class they were going to paint a mural for the library, Marisol couldn't wait to begin.

The classroom buzzed with the sound of brainstorming. The students talked and sketched. Together they made a great big drawing.

Then they marched to the library.
"I'll paint a fish!" "I'll paint one, too."
"I'll paint the ocean!"
Marisol shouted, "I'll paint the sky!"

Marisol rummaged through the box of paint but could not find any blue.

"How am I going to make the sky without blue paint?"

The bell rang. It was time to put their brushes down for the day. As she climbed aboard the bus, Marisol kept wondering.

All the way home, she stared out the window.

The sun lowered closer to the horizon.

Later, at home, Marisol watched
day turn into night.

That night, Marisol settled
into a deep dream.

She drifted through a sky swirling with colors.
The colors mixed, making too many to count.

In the morning, Marisol stood
waiting for the bus in the rain.
The sky was not blue.
She smiled.

At school, Marisol raced to
the library. She grabbed a
dish and began adding colors.
This one, that one. She
swirled the brush to make
an altogether new color.

Marisol then began painting on the wall.
A boy asked, "What color is THAT?"
"That?" Marisol said. "THAT is sky color."

126

Turn and Talk

Use details from **Sky Color** to answer these questions with a partner.

1. **Make Inferences** How does Marisol feel about making the mural? Which details in the text and pictures helped you know?

2. What color does Marisol think the sky is at the beginning of the story? Why does her idea change?

Listening Tip

Listen carefully. Think of questions you want to ask your partner when it is your turn to talk.

Write a TV Commercial

PROMPT Write a TV commercial for the
paint called Sky Color. Tell your opinion of it
and explain ways to use it. Give reasons why
people need it.

PLAN First, fill in the chart with your ideas.
Add details from **Sky Color**.

My Opinion	How to Use It	Why You Need It

WRITE Now write your TV commercial. Make people want to buy this new color of paint! Remember to:

- Use describing words to tell about colors and feelings.

- Use the word **because** to explain your reasons.

_____

- -

_____

- -

_____

- -

_____

- -

_____

- -

_____

- -

_____

- -

_____

Prepare to Read

GENRE STUDY ▶ **Poetry** uses images, sounds, and rhythm to express ideas and feelings. Look for:

- words that rhyme

- words or lines that are repeated

- alliteration, or a pattern of words with the same first sound

POWER WORDS

promise

merrily

SET A PURPOSE ▶ Make pictures in your mind as you read. Words that tell how things look, sound, feel, taste, or smell and words about feelings can help you **create mental images**.

Meet Nikki Grimes.

ME x 2

I read times two.
I write times two.
I think, I dream,
   I cry times two.

I laugh times two.
I'm right times two.
I sing, I ask,
   I try times two.

I do twice as much
   As most people do.
'Cause most speak one,
   But I speak two!

by Jane Medina

The Shoe Rack

by Nikki Grimes

The shoe rack
Is stacked
With promise,

With dreams
Waiting
To wake.

What you do,
Where you go,
Who you grow

134

Up to be
Depends on
The steps you take.

135

Flying-Man

Flying-man, Flying-man,
Up in the sky,
Where are you going to,
Flying so high?

Over the mountains
And over the sea,
Flying-man, Flying-man,
Can't you take me?

Nursery Rhyme

136

Row, Row, Row Your Boat

Row, row, row your boat,
Gently down the stream.
Merrily, merrily, merrily, merrily,
Life is but a dream.

Traditional Song

Star Light, Star Bright

Star light, star bright,
First star I see tonight,
I wish I may, I wish I might,
Have the wish I wish tonight.

Nursery Rhyme

Turn and Talk

Use details from **We Are the Future** to answer these questions with a partner.

1. **Create Mental Images** What do you picture in your mind for each poem? Which of the poets' words help you picture things?

2. What is the main message or the lesson you can learn from each poem?

Talking Tip

Share your own ideas to add on to what your partner says.

My idea about that is _____.

Write an Opinion

PROMPT Think about your future! Which shoe from the poem "The Shoe Rack" shows a job or activity you would most like to do someday? Write to tell why.

PLAN First, draw the shoe. Write four reasons why you would like to do the job or activity.

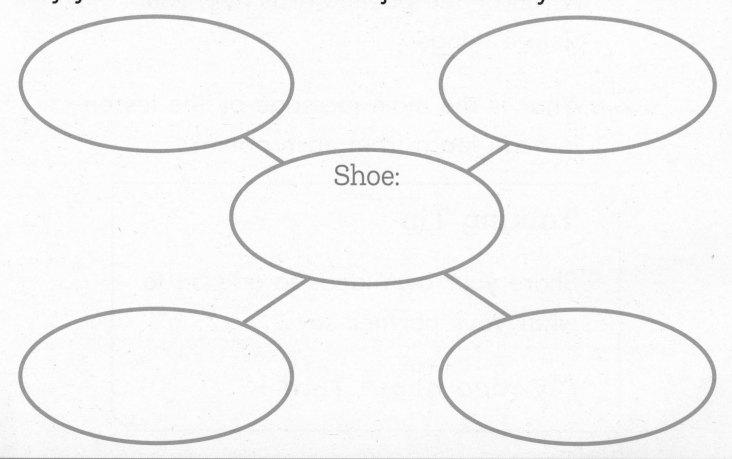

Shoe:

WRITE Now write sentences telling what the job or activity is and why you want to do it someday. Remember to:

- Tell your opinion.

- Use the word **because** to make your reasons clear and strong.

_____

- -

_____

_____

- -

_____

_____

- -

_____

_____

- -

_____

_____

- -

_____

Prepare to Read

GENRE STUDY **Fantasy** stories have made-up events that could not really happen. Look for:

- characters who are not real
- a setting, or where and when the story happens

SET A PURPOSE As you read, **make connections** to find ways that the text is like things in your life and other texts you have read. Compare and contrast to help you understand the text.

Meet Pablo Bernasconi.

JOAQUÍN'S ZOO

BY PABLO BERNASCONI

Joaquín is a **clever boy**. One day, he woke up and had a great idea.

"Today I'm going to build something," he thought.

"I'll use scraps to make **ten animals**
to keep me company."

Joaquín spent day and night in his shop. After a lot of **hard work**, he finished all the animals.

146

He built a hippo out of a cheese grater. Even though he **eats all day**, he never gains any weight.

A feather duster and two twigs make up this **silly guy**. He has messy hair, and he isn't very neat.

Enrique the mouse calls
from an old phone. He
goes *r-i-i-ing* when
he laughs. You can hear
his sound from far,
far away.

This lion with a golden
mane is named Teodoro.
He is **very tame**. In
this jungle, he is king.

He's made up of veggies. No one knows his real name, so he's called Mr. Avocado. His feet are **very fragile**.

This alarm clock is made from a clock and a horn. It **sings in the morning** like an early-rising rooster.

Bortolo the rabbit is made from a lamp and two wheels. He's usually in a **bad mood**, so he's always alone.

Virulana the bird is round and very light. He's **black as night**, so you can't see him when he flies through the dark.

This elephant has a French horn for a trunk. He's **loud when he sings**, and I won't even tell you how loud he is when he snores!

Joaquín worked and worked to put together this giraffe! He used a crane to finish it and a ladder to comb its **unruly hair**.

Joaquín is happy when he finishes. He has **ten new friends** in his garden.

153

His **dream of inventing** has come true. Now they all live together under the same roof!

Turn and Talk

JOAQUÍN'S ZOO
BY PABLO BERNASCONI

Use details from **Joaquín's Zoo** to answer these questions with a partner.

1. **Make Connections** How is Joaquín like Marisol in **Sky Color**? How is what he does different from what Marisol does?

2. Tell about a time you did something like Joaquín, such as make or invent something.

Talking Tip

Ask a question if you are not sure about your partner's ideas.

What did you mean when you said _____?

Write a Letter

PROMPT Write a letter to Joaquín! Tell which animal invention you like best and why. Use details from **Joaquín's Zoo** to explain.

PLAN First, write reasons why you like Joaquín's animal invention. Add questions you want to ask Joaquín.

Why I Like _____	Questions to Ask

WRITE Now write your letter to Joaquín! Tell him why you like the animal invention. Ask him questions about things you want to know. Remember to:

- Give reasons why you like the animal.

- Use the correct end mark for each sentence.

Prepare to View

GENRE STUDY **Videos** are short movies. Some videos give information. Others are for you to watch for enjoyment. Watch and listen for:

• the main topic and details

• how the pictures, words, and sounds work together to give information

SET A PURPOSE Watch the video to find out the **topic** and **central idea** it shares. Look and listen for important details that help you understand it.

Build Background: Inventors

MARCONI
AND THE RADIO
from StoryBots

As You View Find out who the video is about and what he invents. What do people think of his invention at first? What do they think of it later on?

READ
Together

Turn and Talk

MARCONI
AND THE RADIO
from StoryBots

Use details from **Marconi and the Radio** to answer these questions with a partner.

1. **Topic and Central Idea** Think about the video. What is the main thing about Marconi that you learned?

2. How do Marconi's inventions help people?

Listening Tip

Listen carefully. Make connections. How is what your partner is saying like other things you know?

READ
Together

Let's Wrap Up!

? Essential Question

How can thinking in new ways help solve problems?

Pick one of these activities to show what you have learned about the topic.

1. Invent an Animal

Think of an animal to invent, like Joaquín did. Draw a picture of it made from things in your classroom. Write to describe it and what it does.

2. Dreamer's List

Inventors and other people work hard to make their dreams come true. They think of new ideas. What else? Make a list of things to do if you want to make or do new things. Share it!

Word Challenge
Can you use the word future to help explain your ideas?

My Notes

Glossary

A

absorb   When things absorb, they soak something up or take it in. The sponge will **absorb** the spilled water.

applaud   When you applaud something, you clap or show that you like it in some other way. We clapped our hands to **applaud** his great song.

artist   An artist is a person who makes pictures and other art. The **artist** painted a colorful picture.

B

build   When you build something, you make it by putting things together. We can **build** a house with blocks.

C

cook   When you cook, you heat food to get it ready for eating. We use a pan to **cook** food to eat.

D

delicious   When something is delicious, it tastes very good. The fruit tastes so **delicious**!

designed If you designed something, you planned what it will look like when it gets made. We **designed** a cover for our class book.

E

emerge When things emerge, they slowly come out where we can see them. We see the plants after they **emerge** from the soil.

F

floor A floor is one part of a tall building. My family's apartment is on the third **floor**.

future The future is the time that has not happened yet. In the **future**, I want to be a teacher.

G

gallery A gallery is a place where people look at art. We looked at paintings at the art **gallery**.

genius A genius is a very smart person. The person who invented computers was a **genius**.

golden If something is golden, it is a yellow color that looks like gold. The dog has light, **golden** fur.

H

harvest When you harvest foods, you pick and gather them. I picked carrots to help **harvest** the food we grew.

I

indigo Indigo is a color that looks like blue and purple mixed together. **Indigo** thread looks more blue than purple.

ingredients Ingredients are the foods you use or mix together to make other foods. Use tomatoes and other **ingredients** to make a pizza.

J

juicy If something is juicy, it is very wet when you eat it. The **juicy** peach made my hands messy.

M

merrily When you do something merrily, you feel happy. We danced **merrily** to the happy music.

model A model looks the same as a big thing only it is smaller. I made a **model** of the sun and the planets.

mural A mural is a big painting that is often made on a wall. We like the big **mural** painted on the wall.

N

neat If something is neat, it is clean and not messy. We keep our desks **neat** at school.

nutrients Nutrients are things that help plants and animals grow, like food. The plant gets the **nutrients** it needs from the dirt.

P

pounding If you are pounding on something, you are hitting it hard many times. He is **pounding** on the nail with a hammer.

promise If something shows promise, it means something good will probably happen. He shows **promise** of becoming a great soccer player.

R

real If something is real, you can really see it and it is not fake, made up, or pretend. I yelled because the toy spider looked **real**!

ripe If something is ripe, it is finished growing and is ready to eat. The **ripe**, red tomato will taste good.

rummaged If you rummaged, you used your hands to move things around as you looked for something. I **rummaged** through the clothes to find my shirt.

S

scraps Scraps are small pieces that are left over after something is used. The bird used **scraps** of paper to make its nest.

smooth If something is smooth, it is flat and not bumpy. The skin on my arm feels soft and **smooth**.

soil Soil is the dirt that plants live in. We dug holes in the **soil** to plant seeds.

sow When you sow seeds, you put them in the dirt. Let's **sow** corn seeds in our garden.

straight If something is straight, it is not bent or round. Use a ruler to draw a **straight** line.

stretched If something stretched, it became its full size or got even longer or wider. I **stretched** my arm up so I could reach the box.

sturdy If something is sturdy, it is strong. The wind did not blow over the **sturdy** tree.

syrup Syrup is something sweet and sticky that you can pour. I pour **syrup** on my pancakes.

T

terrific If something is terrific, it is great. We clapped at the end of a **terrific** show.

Acknowledgments

Excerpt by Wilma Rudolph from *African American Quotations* by Richard Newman. Published by Chronicle Books. Text copyright © Wilma Rudolph. Reprinted by permission of the Estate of Wilma Rudolph, c/o CMG Worldwide, Inc.

Joaquín's Zoo (retitled from *El Zoo de Joaquín*) by Pablo Bernasconi. Copyright © 2006 by Pablo Bernasconi. Illustration copyright © 2011 by La Brujita de Papel S.A. Reprinted by permission of Kalandraka Ediciones and La Brujita de Papel.

"Me x 2" by Jane Medina from *Amazing Faces* by Lee Bennett Hopkins. Published by Lee & Low Books, Inc. Text copyright © 2010 by Jane Medina. Reprinted by permission of Jane Medina.

"Shoe Rack" by Nikki Grimes. Copyright © 2000 by Nikki Grimes. First appeared in *Shoe Magic*, published by Orchard Books/Scholastic. Reprinted by permission of Curtis Brown, Ltd.

Sky Color by Peter H. Reynolds. Copyright © 2012 by Peter H. Reynolds. Reprinted by permission of Candlewick Press, Somerville, MA and Pippin Properties, Inc.

So You Want to Grow a Taco? by Bridget Heos, illustrated by Daniele Fabbri. Text copyright © 2016 by Amicus Publishing. Illustration copyright © 2016 by Amicus Publishing. Reprinted by permission of Amicus Publishing.

The Talking Vegetables retold by Won-Ldy Paye and Margaret H. Lippert, illustrated by Julie Paschkis. Text copyright © 2006 by Won-Ldy Paye and Margaret H. Lippert. Illustrations copyright © 2006 by Julie Paschkis. Reprinted by arrangement with Henry Holt Books for Young Readers.

Web/Electronic Versions: *The Talking Vegetables* retold by Won-Ldy Paye and Margaret H. Lippert, illustrated by Julie Paschkis. Text copyright © 2006 by Won-Ldy Paye and Margaret H. Lippert. Illustrations copyright © 2006 by Julie Paschkis. Reprinted by arrangement with Henry Holt Books for Young Readers. CAUTION: Users are warned that this work is protected under copyright laws and downloading is strictly prohibited. The right to reproduce or transfer the work via any medium must be secured with Henry Holt and Company.

"Which Part Do We Eat?" by Katherine Ayres from *Ladybug* Magazine, May/June 2011. Text copyright © 2011 by Carus Publishing Company. Reprinted by permission of Cricket Media. All Cricket Media material is copyrighted by Carus Publishing d/b/a Cricket Media, and/or various authors and illustrators. Any commercial use or distribution of material without permission is strictly prohibited. Please visit http://www.cricketmedia.com/info/licensing2 for licensing and http://www.cricketmedia.com for subscriptions.

Young Frank Architect by Frank Viva. Copyright © 2013 by Frank Viva. Reprinted by permission of Charlotte Sheedy Literary Agency and The Museum of Modern Art, New York.

"Blueberry," "Corn," "Pecan," "Prickly Pear," and "Tomato" from *Yum! ¡MmMm! ¡Qué rico!: Americas' Sproutings* by Pat Mora, illustrated by Rafael López. Text copyright © 2007 by Pat Mora. Illustration copyright © 2007 by Rafael López. Reprinted by permission of Lee & Low Books Inc.

Credits

U

usually   If something usually happens, it happens a lot. We **usually** play outside after lunch.

V

vegetation   Plants, trees, and flowers are all kinds of vegetation. At the park, the ground is covered with flowers and other **vegetation**.

W

whole   If you have the whole thing, you have all of it. There was nothing left after we ate the **whole** sandwich.

wonder   A wonder is something that is really great or a big surprise. A big rainbow is a **wonder** to see.

Index of Titles and Authors